# Rise
## and
# Exercise!

## by Tonya Leslie

Wright Group

The McGraw-Hill Companies

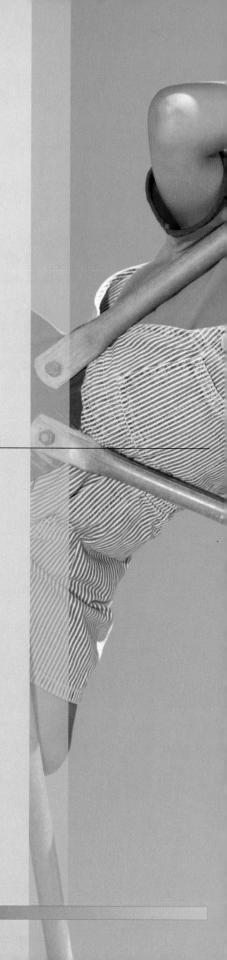

**Photo Credits:**

# www.WrightGroup.com

## Wright Group

Send all inquiries to:
Wright Group/McGraw-Hill
P.O. Box 812960
Chicago, IL 60681

ISBN 978-0-07-658170-2
MHID 0-07-658170-5

4 5 6 7 8 9  DRN  16 15 14 13 12 11

Wake up! Open your eyes!
It's time to rise and exercise!

When you get up, shake off the sleep.
Warm up your muscles by moving
your feet.

Stretch, jump and wiggle,
spin all around. Reach way up high,
touch your hands to the ground.

"Why rise and exercise?" you want to know. One reason is that it helps you to grow.

It builds up your muscles. It makes your bones strong. It gives you energy that lasts all day long!

Exercise is fun! It's just like play.
So don't wait around.
Get started today!

You get exercise when you're at school.
Your brain gets a workout.
Isn't that cool?

But your body needs movement.
That's no surprise.
So at recess, rise and exercise!

Get a friend, or two, three, or four.
Play Simon Says. Then move some more!

Jump like a frog, fly like a plane.
Hop like a bunny, pretend you're a train.

Play Hide and Seek, have relay races.
The playground and gym are
great exercise places.

Sit in a circle for Duck, Duck, Goose.
Round and round—who will he choose?

Don't stop after the school bell rings.
When you get home, you can do
lots of things.

Don't just sit down. That isn't wise.
It's time to rise and exercise!

Turn off the computer.
Leave the TV. There's fun outside,
don't you agree?

Grab a scooter or bike.
Skates are fun too.
Moving around is so good for you!

Call a friend and play catch.
Get a bat and a ball.
Or a game of Freeze Tag is fun for all!

Some kids go to after school care.
They exercise by playing games there.

Doing karate kicks and chops
makes this girl strong.
She hates to stop!

Gymnastics are great exercise, too.
Somersaults are such fun to do!

You can exercise anywhere,
inside or out. Moving your body is
what it's about.

Put on some music and move to the beat. Or go for a walk on a neighborhood street.

What about you? Do you skip and run?
What kind of exercise do you think is fun?

You may like hopscotch or getting a hit.
What do you do to keep yourself fit?

What sports or games do you think
take the prize?
How do YOU rise and exercise?

Let's see now, what did you learn?
Think about each thing in turn.

Exercise is important and lots of fun.
You can exercise anywhere and
with anyone.

Exercise at school and
in your own home.
Join a team or do it alone.

So tell your family and friends,
now that you're wise,
"It's time to rise and exercise!"

WrightGroup.com

The McGraw·Hill Companies

Unit **8** Healthy Food/Healthy Body

ISBN 978007658170-2
MHID 007658170-5

90000

9 780076 581702

McGraw Hill **Education**